News from the Market

by Derek Scott
illustrated by Susy Boyer

SCHOOL PUBLISHERS

Printed in China

ISBN 10: 0-15-350401-3
ISBN 13: 978-0-15-350401-3

Ordering Options
ISBN 10: 0-15-350332-7 (Grade 2 Below-Level Collection)
ISBN 13: 978-0-15-350332-0 (Grade 2 Below-Level Collection)
ISBN 10: 0-15-357428-3 (package of 5)
ISBN 13: 978-0-15-357428-3 (package of 5)

11 12 13 14 15   0940   15 14 13 12 11 10

Characters

Reporter
(Julia)

Anchor I

Anchor 2

Steve
(sells food at
the market)

Producer

Setting: The set of a television newsroom

Producer: Action!

Anchor 1: Good morning. This is City News.

Anchor 2: Today, our reporter Julia is going through the town market. She's asking Steve about the freshest food.

Reporter: This fish looks very fresh, Steve.

Steve: It *is* fresh, Julia. The vegetables are fresh, too. Look at these carrots!

Reporter: They look great! What else is good?

6

Steve: Let's go over to the apples.

Reporter: Okay.

Steve: Apples are a special price today, and I'm sure they taste good. I'm going to eat one to prove it!

Reporter: May I have one, too?

Reporter: It is only eight o'clock, and about a hundred people are here already.

Anchor I: Wow!

Reporter: Everything is selling fast. Sometimes it is all sold by lunchtime!

Anchor 2: Finally, Julia, what is the best thing to buy today?

Reporter: I guess the tomatoes are best. I'm going to buy some!

12

Anchor 1: Thanks, Julia.

Anchor 2: That's the news in our town today.

Producer: Good work!

Think Critically

1. What tells you that this is a Readers' Theater?

2. Who were the characters in the television studio? Who were the characters at the market?

3. Where did the story take place?

4. What was the best thing to buy at the market that day?

5. Which fresh food at the market do you like best? Why?

 **Social Studies**

Write a Paragraph There are apples at the market. Write a paragraph telling about how the apples got to the market. Make sure you start from when the farmer planted the apple seeds.

School-Home Connection Talk to a family member about the book. Then talk about other things you can buy at markets.

Word Count: 187